The Lead Generation Handbook
Sales and Marketing Lead Generation

By Jacob Dunn

Copyright © 2023 Jacob Dunn
All rights reserved.

Table of Contents

Chapter 1: Introduction to Lead Generation 5

1: Introduction to Lead Generation 5

Section 1: What is Lead Generation? 6

Section 2: Benefits of Lead Generation 8

Section 3: Types of Lead Generation 9

Chapter 2: Strategies for Effective Lead Generation 11

2: Strategies for Effective Lead Generation 11

Section 1: Identifying Your Target Audience 12

Section 2: Setting Goals and Objectives 13

Section 3: Creating an Effective Lead Generation Plan 14

Chapter 3: Tools and Resources for Lead Generation 17

3: Tools and Resources for Lead Generation 17

Section 1: Lead Generation Software 18

Section 2: Lead Generation Strategies 19

Section 3: Best Practices for Lead Generation 20

Chapter 4: Measuring Lead Generation Success 23

4: Measuring Lead Generation Success 23

Section 1: Tracking Leads 24

Section 2: Analyzing Lead Quality 26

Section 3: Optimizing Lead Generation Tactics 27

Chapter 5: Lead Nurturing and Conversion 29

5: Lead Nurturing and Conversion 29

Section 1: Creating Lead Nurturing Campaigns 30

Section 2: Optimizing Lead Nurturing Tactics..................................31

Section 3: Strategies for Increasing Lead Conversion...................32

Chapter 6: Lead Generation Tactics..35

6: Lead Generation Tactics 35

Section 1: Content Marketing 36

Section 2: Social Media Marketing..38

Section 3: Pay-Per-Click Advertising 39

Chapter 7: Final Thoughts...41

7: Final Thoughts 41

Section 1: Summary of Lead Generation Strategies......................42

Section 2: Best Practices for Lead Generation 43

Section 3: Tips for Scaling Your Lead Generation Efforts 45

More of our books...47

Chapter 1: Introduction to Lead Generation

Lead generation is the process of attracting and converting prospects into leads, and eventually customers. It involves the identification, acquisition, and nurturing of potential customers for a business. Lead generation tactics include digital marketing, content marketing, email marketing, search engine optimization, and social media marketing. By engaging with potential customers, businesses can build relationships with them, understand their needs, and deliver personalized services to them. Through lead generation, businesses can create a steady stream of leads and revenue over time.

1: Introduction to Lead Generation

Lead generation is the process of acquiring potential customers for a business. It involves identifying, capturing, and nurturing leads to convert them into customers. The goal of lead generation is to build relationships with potential customers and encourage them to purchase a product or service.

Lead generation can be done in many ways, such as through email campaigns, website forms, social media, webinars, search engine optimization, and more. It also involves collecting data about potential customers, such as their contact information and interests, and then using that data to generate leads. Lead generation is an essential part of any successful marketing strategy, as it helps businesses reach out to potential customers.

When starting a lead generation strategy, it's important to focus on creating content that appeals to your target audience. Content should be tailored to the interests of potential customers and should be easy to find and digest. It should also include a call to action that encourages people to take action on the content.

In addition to content, businesses should also focus on building relationships with potential customers. This can be done through email campaigns, social media, and other forms of communication. It's important to engage potential customers and build trust, as this will help increase conversions.

Lead generation also involves tracking and analyzing data about potential customers. Businesses should track which leads are most likely to convert, as well as where they are coming from. This data can then be used to optimize the lead generation strategy and to provide more targeted content to potential customers.

Lead generation is an important part of any business's marketing strategy. It helps businesses reach out to potential customers and build relationships with them. By focusing on creating content that appeals to potential customers and engaging with them, businesses can increase their chances of success. By tracking and analyzing data about potential customers, businesses can also optimize their lead generation strategy and increase conversions.

Section 1: What is Lead Generation?

Lead generation is the process of collecting customer information to identify potential buyers of products and services. It is often done through digital marketing campaigns such as email marketing, search engine marketing, display advertising, social media marketing, and content marketing. These campaigns are designed to capture the interest of potential customers and generate leads for the business.

Lead generation is an important part of the sales process, as it helps businesses identify individuals who may be interested in their products and services. It also helps to develop relationships with potential customers, build brand awareness, and increase sales conversions.

When done correctly, lead generation can be an effective way to generate quality leads. It requires a well-thought-out strategy and the right tactics to help businesses reach their target audience.

To start, businesses must define their target audience. This includes identifying the demographic of potential customers, determining the types of products or services they are interested in, and understanding their needs and wants.

Once the target audience is identified, businesses can create a lead generation campaign that focuses on reaching those people. They can use a variety of tactics such as email marketing, search engine marketing, display advertising, social media marketing, and content marketing.

Email marketing is a great way to reach potential customers. It allows businesses to send targeted emails to a specific list of potential customers. This is a great way to stay top of mind with potential customers and to build relationships.

Search engine marketing allows businesses to make sure their website appears at the top of search engine results for relevant keywords. This helps them reach more potential customers and build brand awareness.

Display advertising is another effective way to reach potential customers. Through display ads, businesses can target potential customers with relevant ads based on their browsing behavior and interests.

Social media marketing is an effective way to reach potential customers. Businesses can explore different platforms to find potential customers and build relationships with them. This can also be used to increase brand awareness and generate leads.

Content marketing is also an effective lead generation strategy. Businesses can create content that educates potential customers about their products and services. This helps to build relationships and trust with potential customers and can result in more leads.

Overall, lead generation is an important part of the sales process. It helps businesses identify potential customers, build relationships, and increase sales conversions. By defining their target audience and using the right tactics, businesses can create successful lead generation campaigns and start generating quality leads.

Section 2: Benefits of Lead Generation

Lead generation is an important part of modern business marketing and sales strategies. It is the process of identifying and compelling potential customers to take action and become prospects for a company's products or services. Lead generation can be achieved through a variety of methods, such as email campaigns, social media marketing, content marketing, pay-per-click advertising, search engine optimization, and more. There are many benefits to lead generation, and we'll discuss a few of them here.

1. Increased Sales: Lead generation helps to increase sales by increasing the number of potential customers who are exposed to a company's offerings. Generating leads is an effective way to build a customer base, and it can also increase sales by improving the quality of the leads. By targeting the right audience, companies can ensure that the leads they generate are more likely to be interested in the company's offerings and more likely to convert into paying customers.

2. Improved Brand Awareness: Lead generation can also help to build brand awareness. By targeting potential customers through various methods, companies can ensure that their brand is seen by the right audience. This can help to increase recognition of the brand and encourage potential customers to learn more about the company and its offerings.

3. Reduced Cost: Lead generation can reduce marketing costs by eliminating the need to target a broad audience. By targeting potential customers who are more likely to be interested in a company's

offerings, companies can ensure that their marketing efforts are more efficient and cost-effective.

4. Improved Customer Relations: Lead generation can also help to improve customer relationships by providing companies with more insight into customer interests and preferences. Companies can use this information to tailor their offerings and provide more personalized customer experiences.

These are just a few of the benefits of lead generation. By identifying and targeting potential customers, companies can ensure that their offerings are seen by the right people and increase their sales. Lead generation can also help to reduce marketing costs, build brand awareness, and improve customer relationships. All of these factors can contribute to the overall success of a company's marketing and sales strategies.

Section 3: Types of Lead Generation

Lead generation is the process of acquiring potential customers or clients for your business. It's a critical part of any marketing strategy and can significantly help your business grow. There are numerous ways to generate leads, but it's important to know which methods are most effective for your business.

The three most common types of lead generation are inbound, outbound, and social media marketing.

Inbound lead generation is when you create content that attracts potential customers. This includes blog posts, infographics, webinars, e-books, and other forms of content. The idea is that potential customers will find your content through search engines or social media, and then click through to your website.

Outbound lead generation is when you reach out directly to potential customers. This usually involves cold calling, emailing, or sending direct mail. The goal is to connect with potential customers and inform them about your business, product, or service.

Social media lead generation is the process of using social media channels to attract potential customers. This includes creating content that is engaging and shareable, as well as leveraging influencers to help amplify your message.

No matter which type of lead generation you choose, it's important to have a clear plan in place and track your results. Set goals for each lead generation tactic and measure the success of each one. This will help you determine which ones are working and which ones need to be improved.

Lead generation can be a powerful tool for businesses of all sizes. It's important to understand the different types of lead generation and how to use them effectively in order to generate the most leads and convert them into customers. With the right strategies, you can successfully generate leads and grow your business.

Lead generation is the process of identifying and attracting potential customers to your business. It's an important part of any marketing strategy and can help you build relationships with potential customers, increase sales, and grow your business. Chapter 1: Introduction to Lead Generation covers the basics of lead generation, including understanding the target audience, creating a lead generation strategy, and utilizing the right tools and techniques. Additionally, this chapter will discuss the importance of tracking, analyzing, and optimizing lead generation efforts in order to ensure maximum success. With the right tactics, lead generation can be an invaluable asset to any business.

Chapter 2: Strategies for Effective Lead Generation

Chapter 2 of "Lead Generation Strategies" provides valuable tips and advice on how to successfully generate leads. It covers topics such as developing a customer-centric approach, understanding customer needs, and effective use of technology and digital marketing. It also discusses the importance of optimizing websites and landing pages, as well as the importance of creating compelling content and using social media to reach target audiences. Additionally, it covers lead nurturing, lead scoring, and data analysis techniques. By following the strategies outlined in this chapter, businesses can generate quality leads that can be converted into profitable customers.

2: Strategies for Effective Lead Generation

Lead generation is the process of identifying and capturing potential customer interest in a product or service. An effective lead generation strategy is essential for any business to grow and increase their customer base. Here are two strategies for effective lead generation that can be used by businesses of all sizes.

The first strategy is content marketing. Content marketing is the process of creating and distributing content that attracts and engages potential customers. This can include blog posts, ebooks, videos, white papers, webinars, or any other type of content that is relevant to the business's target audience. Content marketing is a great way to build relationships with potential customers and to get them interested in what the business has to offer.

The second strategy is social media marketing. Social media marketing is the process of using social media platforms to promote a business's products or services. This includes creating content such as images, videos, and stories, and engaging with potential customers on platforms such as Facebook, Instagram, Twitter, and LinkedIn. Social media marketing is a great way to reach a wide audience and to increase brand awareness.

Both content marketing and social media marketing are effective methods of lead generation. Content marketing can be used to educate potential customers about a business's offerings and to build relationships with them. Social media marketing can be used to reach a wider audience and to increase brand awareness. By leveraging both strategies, businesses can create a comprehensive lead generation plan that will help them grow their customer base.

Lead generation is essential for any business to succeed. By leveraging content marketing and social media marketing, businesses can create an effective lead generation strategy that will help them grow their customer base. With the right plan in place, businesses can generate quality leads that will help them increase their revenue and grow their business.

Section 1: Identifying Your Target Audience

Identifying your target audience is essential for any successful business. Doing so can help you tailor your product or service to meet the needs of your customers, as well as helping you better understand your market and how to reach them.

When it comes to identifying your target audience, it's important to consider the demographic characteristics of your customers. This includes factors like age, gender, income level, occupation, location, and interests. Knowing the demographic characteristics of your customers can help you tailor your product or service to meet their specific needs.

It's also important to consider the psychographic characteristics of your customers. This includes factors such as lifestyle, values, attitudes, interests, and beliefs. Understanding these characteristics can help you create content and marketing messages that resonate with your target audience.

Another important factor to consider is the behavior of your target audience. This includes factors such as how often they purchase, what type of products or services they buy, and where they shop. Knowing the behavior of your customers can help you create an effective marketing strategy.

It's also important to understand the needs and preferences of your target audience. This includes factors such as what type of product or service they need, their price range, and their preferences for certain features. Knowing this information can help you create a product or service that meets the needs of your target audience.

Finally, it's important to consider the media habits of your target audience. This includes factors such as what type of media they consume, which channels they use, and which devices they use. Knowing this information can help you create an effective digital marketing strategy that reaches your target audience.

Identifying your target audience is essential for any successful business. Taking the time to understand the demographic, psychographic, behavioral, and media habits of your target audience can help you create an effective marketing strategy that resonates with them. Doing so can help you reach more of your target audience, increase sales, and grow your business.

Section 2: Setting Goals and Objectives

Setting goals and objectives is an essential part of any successful business or organization. Goals provide direction and motivation, while objectives provide specific steps for achieving those goals. By setting goals and objectives, you can create a plan of action that will help you reach your desired outcome.

The first step in setting goals and objectives is to identify the desired outcome. What do you hope to achieve? This will be the basis for all of your goals and objectives.

Once you have identified the desired outcome, you need to create specific goals and objectives that will help you reach that outcome. Goals should be measurable and attainable. For example, if your goal is to increase sales, you need to set specific goals for sales increases in certain markets or timeframes. Objectives should be specific, actionable steps that will help you achieve those goals. For example, if your goal is to increase sales in a certain market, your objectives could include developing a marketing plan, targeting specific customers, and improving customer service.

You also need to set deadlines for achieving these goals and objectives. Deadlines help to keep you on track and give you a sense of urgency. Without deadlines, it is easy to get sidetracked or procrastinate.

Once you have set goals and objectives, you need to create a plan of action. This plan should include how you will reach each goal and objective, as well as who is responsible for each task. You also need to establish a timeline for reaching your goals and objectives.

Finally, you need to track your progress. This is essential for making sure you are on track and for identifying any areas that need improvement. You should review your progress regularly to ensure that you are on track and making progress towards your goals and objectives.

Setting goals and objectives is a critical part of any successful business or organization. By setting measurable goals and actionable objectives, and creating a plan of action, you can ensure that you are on track to reach your desired outcome. With a timeline and regular progress reviews, you can stay focused and motivated to reach your goals and objectives.

Section 3: Creating an Effective Lead Generation Plan

Lead generation is a critical part of growing any business. It is the process of attracting and converting prospects into paying customers. A successful lead generation plan requires an effective strategy, as well as the right tools and resources to maximize the effectiveness of the effort.

First, it is important to identify the target audience for the lead generation plan. Consider the demographic characteristics of those who are most likely to purchase the product or service, such as age, gender, location, and income level. This will help to narrow the focus and ensure that the lead generation plan is tailored to the right people.

Once the target audience is known, the next step is to create a compelling message that will draw them in. This can be done through a combination of content marketing, social media, and email campaigns. Content marketing is an effective way to reach potential customers through informative blog posts, videos, and other forms of content that can be shared across multiple channels. Social media is another great way to reach the target audience, as it is a great platform for creating relationships and building trust. Finally, email campaigns can be used to nurture relationships, build trust, and engage with prospects.

The next step is to create a way to track and measure the results of the lead generation plan. This can be done through the use of analytics and reporting tools that can provide valuable insights into the effectiveness of the plan. These tools can also provide data on the number of leads generated, the conversion rate, and the average revenue generated from each lead.

Finally, it is important to continually refine the lead generation plan. This can be done by testing different messages and approaches to ensure that the plan is as effective as possible. Additionally, it is important to stay up to date on the latest trends and technologies, as well as competitor activities, to ensure that the lead generation plan remains effective and is able to keep up with the changing landscape.

Creating an effective lead generation plan requires effort and dedication. By focusing on the target audience and creating a compelling message, tracking and measuring the results, and staying up to date on the latest trends and technologies, businesses can create a successful lead generation plan that will help to grow their business.

Chapter 2 of "Lead Generation Strategies" focuses on the importance of developing and implementing effective lead generation strategies. It outlines the importance of segmenting leads, understanding the customer journey, and utilizing digital marketing tactics to capture leads. It also covers the importance of using data-driven insights to gain insights into potential customers and develop targeted campaigns. The chapter also covers how to measure the success of lead generation campaigns, and how to use a variety of techniques to create and nurture leads. By using these strategies, businesses can increase their lead conversion rate and grow their customer base.

Chapter 3: Tools and Resources for Lead Generation

In Chapter 3 of the book, Tools and Resources for Lead Generation, readers learn how to use digital tools and resources to generate leads, such as CRM systems, email automation, and social media. These tools provide a comprehensive system for capturing and nurturing leads, so businesses can reach out to potential customers and build relationships. Additionally, the chapter covers how to measure lead performance, and how to select and prioritize leads to make the most of the resources available. Overall, the chapter provides an in-depth understanding of the best tools and resources for lead generation.

3: Tools and Resources for Lead Generation

Lead generation is essential for any business that wants to grow and succeed. It's the process of identifying potential customers and convincing them to purchase your products or services.

To help you generate leads, there are many tools and resources available. Here are three of the most powerful ones:

1. Social Media Platforms – Social media is one of the most powerful ways to generate leads. It allows you to build relationships with potential customers and engage with them on a personal level. You can use social media platforms such as Facebook, Twitter, and Instagram to promote your business and capture leads. Just make sure you create content that resonates with your target audience.

2. Email Marketing – Email marketing is another effective tool for lead generation. It allows you to capture the email addresses of potential customers and send them relevant information about your business. You can also use email marketing to nurture leads and develop relationships with them. To make the most of it, use segmentation to target the right customers and create personalized messages.

3. Landing Pages – Landing pages are essential for capturing leads.

They are designed to capture the information of visitors who are interested in your product or service. You can use landing pages to offer free downloads, discounts, or other incentives to encourage visitors to sign up. Make sure your landing pages are optimized for conversions and provide a clear call-to-action.

These are just three of the many tools and resources you can use for lead generation. Make sure you take advantage of them to capture the leads you need to grow your business. With the right approach, you can generate high-quality leads and turn them into customers.

Section 1: Lead Generation Software

Lead Generation Software is an essential tool for businesses of any size. It simplifies the process of capturing leads and automates the process of converting them into customers. Lead generation software is used to collect contact information from prospective customers and can be used to reach them with marketing messages, offer discounts, and more.

Lead generation software helps businesses to automate the process of capturing leads and converting them into customers. It can be used to generate leads from various sources, such as search engine optimization (SEO), pay-per-click (PPC) campaigns, email marketing, and social media. The software can also be used to create custom forms, surveys, polls, and quizzes to capture leads and convert them into customers.

Lead generation software can be used to target specific demographics, including age, gender, location, and interests. This allows businesses to tailor their campaigns to the target audience. The software also helps businesses to track and monitor leads, allowing them to see which campaigns are working and which are not.

Lead generation software also helps businesses to improve their customer service. It can be used to create automated emails and messages, as well as customer service forms, which can help customers quickly get the answers they need. It can also be used to collect customer feedback and reviews, which can help businesses to improve their services.

Overall, lead generation software is an invaluable tool for businesses of any size. It simplifies the process of capturing leads and converting them into customers and can be used to target specific demographics. It also helps businesses to improve their customer service and monitor leads to ensure that their campaigns are effective. By using lead generation software, businesses can ensure that they are reaching the right people at the right time and with the right message.

Section 2: Lead Generation Strategies

Lead generation is the process of identifying potential customers and capturing their contact information in order to create a database of leads for sales and marketing teams to pursue. It involves generating interest in a product or service that will result in sales. The goal is to find individuals who are likely to become paying customers.

Lead generation strategies can involve a variety of tactics, including digital marketing, content marketing, referral marketing, and email marketing.

Digital Marketing

Digital marketing is a great way to generate leads. It involves using online channels, such as search engine optimization (SEO), social media, and email marketing, to promote products or services. SEO involves optimizing web pages for specific keywords and phrases to make them easier for search engines to find. Social media can be used to build relationships with potential customers and create brand awareness. Companies can also use email campaigns to reach out to potential customers with relevant content.

Content Marketing

Content marketing is another effective lead generation strategy. It involves creating quality content, such as blog posts, videos, and podcasts, to educate potential customers about a product or service. Content can be used to build relationships with potential customers by providing them with helpful information. Companies can also use content to drive organic traffic to their websites, which can result in more leads.

Referral Marketing

Referral marketing is another great lead generation strategy. It involves asking existing customers to refer their friends and family to your business. Referrals can be an effective way to generate leads, as it leverages the trust that existing customers have in your business. Companies can also offer incentives to customers who refer others, such as discounts or rewards.

Email Marketing

Email marketing is a powerful lead generation strategy. It involves sending emails to potential customers to promote a product or service. Companies can use email to nurture leads, build relationships, and drive conversions. It is an effective way to reach potential customers, as it is more personal than other forms of marketing.

Lead generation strategies can be used to increase sales and build relationships with potential customers. Digital marketing, content marketing, referral marketing, and email marketing are all effective ways to generate leads. Companies should use a combination of these strategies to maximize their lead generation efforts.

Section 3: Best Practices for Lead Generation

Lead generation is one of the most important elements of successful marketing. It involves the process of collecting contact information from potential customers who may be interested in a company's products or services. When done correctly, lead generation can result in increased sales and ultimately, more revenue.

Here are three best practices for lead generation that marketers should keep in mind:

1. Utilize Multiple Channels

Don't limit yourself to just one or two lead generation channels. Instead, create an integrated approach to lead generation that includes multiple channels such as email, search engine marketing, content marketing, social media, referral programs, and more. This will ensure that you are reaching a wide variety of potential customers.

2. Focus on Quality Over Quantity

When it comes to lead generation, quality is more important than quantity. It's better to have fewer leads that are qualified and highly interested in your product or service than a large number of leads who may not be interested at all. Make sure that your lead generation efforts are focused on collecting data and contact information from people who are likely to be interested in what you have to offer.

3. Embrace Automation

Lead generation can be a time-consuming process, but there are ways to automate parts of it. Utilize technology to help streamline the process and save time. Automation can also help you better target potential customers and ensure that your lead generation efforts are more successful.

Lead generation is an essential part of any successful marketing strategy. By utilizing multiple channels, focusing on quality over quantity, and embracing automation, marketers can ensure that their lead generation efforts are successful. With the right approach, lead generation can result in increased sales and ultimately, more revenue.

Chapter 3 of "The Ultimate Guide to Lead Generation" covers the various tools and resources available to help businesses and marketers generate leads. It identifies different lead generation strategies, such as content marketing, search engine optimization, and email marketing. It also looks at the different tools and technologies that are available, such as automation software and analytics tools. Finally, the chapter provides advice on how to use the tools and resources to maximize lead generation. With the right tools and resources, businesses and marketers can maximize their lead generation efforts and increase their chances of success.

Chapter 4: Measuring Lead Generation Success

Chapter 4 of Lead Generation for Dummies focuses on how to measure the success of your lead generation efforts. It covers topics such as tracking leads, setting goals, and creating detailed reports to track your progress. It also provides tips on how to measure the effectiveness of various lead generation tactics such as email campaigns, paid search ads, and social media campaigns. Additionally, it explores how to measure ROI, including how to track revenue earned from leads generated. Ultimately, the chapter provides valuable insight into how to measure the success of your lead generation efforts and provides actionable advice for optimizing lead generation strategies.

4: Measuring Lead Generation Success

Lead generation is an important part of any business's success. It's the process of attracting and converting potential customers into paying customers. Without lead generation, it's difficult to find and keep customers, which will ultimately lead to a decrease in sales. To ensure that your lead generation efforts are successful, it's essential to measure your progress.

To measure the success of your lead generation efforts, you need to track key performance indicators (KPIs). These are metrics that help you measure the success of your lead generation efforts. Here are some examples of KPIs you should be tracking:

• Lead volume: The number of leads you generate. This can be tracked using your website analytics, email marketing campaigns, or other methods of lead capture.

• Lead conversion rate: This is the percentage of leads that are converted into paying customers.

• Cost per lead: This is the cost associated with acquiring each lead, including advertising, content marketing, and other outreach activities.

- Customer acquisition cost: This is the cost associated with acquiring each customer, including the cost of lead acquisition as well as the cost of nurturing and converting the lead.

- Lifetime value: This is the total amount of money a customer spends with your business over the entire lifetime of their relationship.

These KPIs will help you measure the success of your lead generation efforts. By tracking them, you'll be able to determine which strategies are working and which need to be improved.

You should also track the success of your lead generation campaigns. This can be done by looking at the performance of each individual campaign. Analyze the results of the campaigns to determine which ones are generating the most leads and conversions. This will help you determine which campaigns are most effective and which ones need to be improved.

Finally, it's important to measure the success of your lead nurturing efforts. This includes tracking the number of leads that have been nurtured and the success rate of those leads. This will help you determine which strategies are working and which need to be improved.

Measuring the success of your lead generation efforts is essential for long-term success. It will help you understand which strategies are working and which need to be improved. By tracking key performance indicators and analyzing the success of your campaigns, you'll be able to ensure that your lead generation efforts are successful.

Section 1: Tracking Leads

Lead tracking is an important part of any successful marketing campaign. By tracking leads, businesses can better understand their customers, identify areas for improvement, and maximize their return on investment.

Lead tracking is the process of collecting and analyzing data related to the customer journey from initial contact to purchase or conversion. It involves tracking the customer's activities, such as website visits, online searches, email opens, and more. This data can be used to gain insights into customer behavior and preferences, as well as identify opportunities for improvement.

When setting up tracking for leads, it's important to be mindful of the customer's privacy and ensure that any collected data is secure and used responsibly. Additionally, businesses should be aware of the various legal and ethical considerations related to customer data collection and use.

Lead tracking can be done manually or with the help of automated lead tracking software. Manual tracking requires a lot of time and can be tedious. Automated lead tracking software is more efficient and can automate tasks such as contact list segmentation and lead scoring.

Lead tracking can provide valuable insights into customer behavior and help businesses better understand their customers. It can also provide valuable data on the effectiveness of different marketing campaigns, allowing businesses to optimize their efforts and maximize return on investment.

Lead tracking can also help businesses identify areas for improvement. For example, if a business notices that a certain type of customer is not visiting their website or engaging with their emails, they can use lead tracking data to identify potential opportunities to improve their marketing efforts.

Lead tracking is an important part of any successful marketing campaign. By tracking leads, businesses can better understand their customers, identify areas for improvement, and maximize their return on investment. With the right approach, lead tracking can provide invaluable data and insights that can help businesses make more informed decisions and drive more sales.

Section 2: Analyzing Lead Quality

Lead quality is a critical factor in the success of any business. It is the measure of the ability of leads to become customers and generate revenue for the company. Companies must analyze lead quality to ensure that they are targeting the right prospects and making the most of their marketing efforts.

To analyze lead quality, companies must first determine the source of their leads. Are they coming from organic sources such as social media, or are they from paid sources such as PPC campaigns? Determining the source of the leads can help companies understand how to best target their marketing efforts and ensure that they are reaching the right audiences.

Once the source of the leads is identified, companies must then assess the quality of the leads. This can be done by evaluating the lead's characteristics such as demographics, interests, and behavior. Companies should also measure the response rate to their marketing campaigns and assess how effective their messaging has been in converting leads into customers.

Companies must also ensure that leads are being tracked and monitored over time. This includes monitoring the lead's engagement with the company's content and messaging, as well as tracking their progress from being a lead to becoming a customer. By tracking leads over time, companies can get a better understanding of which marketing efforts are most effective in converting leads into customers.

Finally, companies should use lead scoring to assess the quality of the leads. Lead scoring assigns a numerical value to each lead based on their characteristics and engagement with the company's content. This allows companies to quickly identify the most qualified leads and prioritize their outreach efforts accordingly.

Lead quality is an important metric for any business, and companies must be diligent in assessing and analyzing the quality of their leads. By understanding the source of their leads, assessing the lead's characteristics, tracking their progress, and using lead scoring to prioritize engagement, businesses can ensure that they are targeting the right prospects and making the most of their marketing efforts.

Section 3: Optimizing Lead Generation Tactics

Lead generation tactics are an essential part of any business's marketing strategy. From email campaigns to social media outreach, lead generation tactics are designed to help businesses find potential customers and build relationships with them. By optimizing these tactics, businesses can boost their lead generation efforts and increase their conversion rates.

One way to optimize lead generation tactics is to focus on creating customer-centric content. Quality content that resonates with the target audience can help businesses build trust and credibility, which can result in more leads. Additionally, businesses should ensure that content is tailored to the needs of their target audience, as this can increase engagement and lead to more conversions.

Another way to optimize lead generation tactics is through the use of automated marketing tools. Automated marketing tools can help businesses streamline their lead generation process by automating certain tasks, such as sending emails and generating personalized content. This can help businesses save time and money while also increasing the effectiveness of their lead generation efforts.

Finally, businesses should focus on building relationships with their leads. By engaging with leads on a regular basis, businesses can start building relationships and increase the likelihood of converting leads into customers. This can be done by sending customized emails, offering discounts and incentives, and providing helpful content.

By optimizing lead generation tactics, businesses can increase their chances of converting leads into customers. By focusing on creating customer-centric content, leveraging automated marketing tools, and building relationships with leads, businesses can boost their lead generation efforts and increase their conversion rates. In turn, businesses can maximize their return on investment and gain a competitive edge in the marketplace.

In Chapter 4 of Lead Generation, authors discuss how to measure success. They recommend tracking metrics such as number of leads generated, conversion rate, and cost per lead. Additionally, they suggest tracking key performance indicators like click-through rate, cost per click, and time on page to gauge engagement with content. Ultimately, the authors emphasize the importance of having a clear understanding of the desired outcome when launching a lead generation campaign to ensure that the right metrics are tracked to measure success. They also highlight the importance of using the data to adjust campaigns in order to reach the desired outcome.

Chapter 5: Lead Nurturing and Conversion

Lead nurturing and conversion is essential to any successful marketing strategy. This chapter discusses how to nurture leads into customers through effective communication and targeted marketing. It outlines a variety of techniques, such as email campaigns, content marketing, and remarketing, that can be used to nurture leads and turn them into customers. It also covers ways to measure conversion rates and monitor progress. Ultimately, lead nurturing and conversion are essential components of any successful marketing strategy, and this chapter provides readers with an in-depth understanding of how to ensure that their campaign is successful.

5: Lead Nurturing and Conversion

Lead nurturing and conversion is the process of turning prospects into customers. It involves developing relationships with potential customers to convert them into paying customers. It's about building trust and credibility with prospects to eventually close the sale.

Lead nurturing is a key component of any successful sales strategy. It is the process of engaging potential customers throughout their journey from discovering your brand to eventually becoming a paying customer. It is not a one-time event, but rather a continuous process that involves nurturing leads through personalized and timely messages.

Lead nurturing can take many forms, such as email campaigns, personalization, targeted content, and drip campaigns. Each of these strategies is designed to move leads down the sales funnel and convert them into customers.

Email campaigns are a great way to stay in touch with prospects. They can be used to send personalized messages, educational content, and promotional offers. Personalization can also be used to send messages that are tailored to each individual prospect. Targeted content can be used to provide relevant information that is tailored to each prospect's needs. Finally, drip campaigns can be used to send a series of emails over a period of time.

In addition to lead nurturing, conversion optimization is also important. Conversion optimization is the process of improving the conversion rate of your website. This process includes testing different elements of your website, such as headlines, images, and copy, to see which ones are most effective at converting visitors into customers.

Lead nurturing and conversion optimization are both essential components of any successful sales strategy. Lead nurturing helps to build relationships with prospects and move them down the sales funnel. Conversion optimization focuses on optimizing the elements of your website to increase the conversion rate. By implementing both strategies, you can maximize the effectiveness of your sales process and increase your overall sales.

Section 1: Creating Lead Nurturing Campaigns

Lead nurturing is the process of developing relationships with potential buyers over time. It involves creating and delivering personalized content to prospects at different stages of the buyer's journey. Lead nurturing campaigns are an essential component of a successful marketing strategy as they help to convert more leads into customers.

Lead nurturing campaigns should be tailored to the individual needs of each prospect. This means understanding who your target audience is, what they need, and when they need it. It also requires creating content that speaks to their interests and goals.

When creating a lead nurturing campaign, it's important to start by determining what content you'll be providing to prospects. This could include blog posts, ebooks, videos, or webinars. The content should be engaging and informative, and it should be tailored to the individual needs of each prospect.

Once you've identified the content you'll be providing, it's time to create a timeline for the campaign. This should include when the content will be sent out, how often it will be sent, and what type of response you want to see from the prospect.

It's also important to set up a system for tracking and measuring the success of the lead nurturing campaign. This will help you determine what content is working and what needs to be tweaked.

Finally, it's important to ensure that you're providing prospects with an opportunity to take action. You can do this by providing them with a call to action, such as signing up for a newsletter or downloading an ebook. This will help to further engage prospects and move them further down the funnel.

Lead nurturing campaigns are an essential part of any successful marketing strategy. By providing prospects with personalized content and an opportunity to take action, you can convert more leads into customers. By tracking and measuring the success of the campaign, you can continually refine and improve your lead nurturing efforts.

Section 2: Optimizing Lead Nurturing Tactics

Lead nurturing is an essential part of any successful marketing strategy. It helps build relationships with potential customers and leads them through the sales funnel until they're ready to make a purchase. To make sure lead nurturing is effective, it's important to optimize tactics and measure their success.

One way to optimize lead nurturing tactics is to focus on personalization. Rather than sending generic messages to everyone in your database, create content tailored to specific customer segments. This way, you can make sure the content you're sending is relevant to each individual. Make sure to include customer data like demographics, purchase history, and interests in order to personalize your content.

Another way to optimize lead nurturing tactics is to use A/B testing.

A/B testing allows you to test different versions of your content to see which one performs better. It's important to test different messages, calls-to-action, and design elements to make sure you're getting the best results.

Finally, it's important to measure the success of your lead nurturing tactics. You can do this by looking at metrics like open rates, click-through rates, and conversion rates. If you're not seeing the results you want, it might be time to change up your tactics.

By optimizing lead nurturing tactics, you can ensure that your campaigns are as effective as possible. Make sure to personalize content, use A/B testing, and measure your results to make sure you're reaching the right people in the most effective way. Doing so will help you get the most out of your lead nurturing efforts.

Section 3: Strategies for Increasing Lead Conversion

Lead conversion is a key element in any business's success. It is the process of turning leads into paying customers. Without it, businesses cannot grow and generate revenue. Fortunately, there are a number of strategies that can be used to increase lead conversion rates.

The first strategy is to focus on personalization. Personalizing content and messages to each lead can make prospects feel appreciated and valued. It also shows that the business is paying attention and is genuinely interested in helping them solve their problems. Companies can use AI-driven marketing platforms to personalize emails, web pages, and other forms of communication based on customer data.

The second strategy is to use omnichannel marketing. Omnichannel marketing involves using multiple channels to reach out to potential customers. This could include email, website, social media, SMS, and more. By using multiple channels, businesses can increase their chances of connecting with leads and forming relationships.

The third strategy is to use lead nurturing tactics. Lead nurturing is a process of actively engaging with leads in order to build relationships and move them further down the sales funnel. This could include sending out emails, setting up automated campaigns, or hosting webinars. By staying in contact with leads, businesses can ensure that they don't forget about them or miss out on potential opportunities.

The fourth strategy is to use lead scoring. Lead scoring is a process of assigning a numerical value to leads based on their likelihood of converting. Businesses can use lead scoring to identify which leads are most likely to purchase and prioritize them accordingly. This helps to ensure that resources are used efficiently and that sales teams are focusing on the right leads.

The fifth strategy is to optimize the customer journey. By understanding the customer journey, businesses can identify any potential points of friction and address them accordingly. This could involve making it easier for customers to find the right information, streamlining the checkout process, or providing additional customer support.

Lead conversion is an essential part of business success. By implementing the above strategies, businesses can increase their lead conversion rates and maximize their return on investment. Optimizing the customer journey, focusing on personalization, using omnichannel marketing, lead nurturing, and lead scoring are all strategies that can be used to increase lead conversion.

Lead nurturing and conversion are key steps in the marketing funnel. Lead nurturing is the process of developing relationships with potential customers, while conversion is when a lead becomes a customer. Lead nurturing involves creating personalized content to build trust and encourage prospects to take action. Conversion requires an effective strategy and a great product or service. It's important to track and monitor leads to discover what works and what doesn't in order to optimize the user experience. With a clear understanding of the customer journey, businesses can optimize their lead nurturing and conversion strategies to maximize sales and revenue.

Chapter 6: Lead Generation Tactics

Chapter 6 of the book discusses lead generation tactics. It covers a variety of tactics that can be used to generate leads, such as using search engine optimization, leveraging social media, creating content marketing campaigns, and creating an email list. It also provides insight into what types of content are most effective for lead generation, as well as how to measure the success of lead generation efforts. Ultimately, the chapter provides readers with a comprehensive overview of the various lead generation tactics that can be used to attract potential customers.

6: Lead Generation Tactics

Lead generation is an essential part of any successful business. It involves attracting potential customers to your products or services and converting them into leads. Without leads, you won't have any customers. Here are six lead generation tactics that can help you grow your business.

1. Content Marketing: Content marketing is a great way to get people interested in your business. Create content that's helpful, interesting, and informative. This can range from blog posts to videos to podcasts. The more helpful and engaging your content is, the more likely people will be to interact with it and become leads.

2. Paid Ads: Paid ads can be a great way to instantly increase your visibility online and attract new leads. You can use platforms like Google Ads or Facebook Ads to reach potential customers. Make sure to create ads that are targeted and engaging to ensure that you're getting the most out of your ad spend.

3. Social Media: Social media is a great way to build relationships and connect with potential leads. Post content regularly and engage with your followers. Ask questions, start conversations, and share valuable content to attract new leads.

4. Email Marketing: Email is still one of the most effective ways to

reach customers. Create an email list and send out regular emails with useful content and offers. Make sure to personalize your emails and create a compelling subject line to increase the chances of it being opened and read.

5. Networking: Networking is a great way to meet potential leads in person. Attend conferences, mixers, and other events in your industry. This will give you an opportunity to make connections and potentially generate leads.

6. Referrals: Referrals are one of the most effective ways to generate leads. Ask your current customers to refer you to their friends and family. Offer incentives such as discounts or free products to encourage them to do so.

These are just a few of the lead generation tactics that can help you grow your business. Implementing each of these strategies will help you attract more leads and ultimately increase your customer base. By focusing on lead generation, you'll be able to build relationships with potential customers and grow your business.

Section 1: Content Marketing

Content marketing is a strategic approach that focuses on creating and distributing valuable, relevant, and consistent content to attract and retain a clearly defined audience with the goal of driving profitable customer action. Content marketing is a powerful tool for businesses of all sizes and industries, and it is important for businesses to understand the benefits of content marketing and how to implement it effectively.

Content marketing is an effective way to reach potential customers and build relationships with them. By providing content that is interesting and informative, businesses can engage their audience and create a loyal following. Content marketing can also help businesses build trust with their customers, as well as educate them on the products and services they offer.

Content marketing can be used to promote products and services, increase brand awareness, and drive sales. By creating content that is valuable and relevant, businesses can increase their visibility and reach more potential customers. Additionally, content marketing can be used to engage customers and build relationships with them. By providing content that is informative and entertaining, businesses can create an emotional connection with their audience and increase customer loyalty.

Content marketing is also a great way to increase website traffic. Creating content that is interesting and relevant to your target audience can help you attract more visitors to your website. Additionally, content marketing can be used to improve your search engine rankings, as search engines prioritize content that is relevant and informative.

Content marketing is an essential part of any marketing strategy. It is important to create content that is engaging, interesting, and relevant to your target audience. Additionally, it is important to create content that is consistent and regularly updated so that your audience is engaged and informed. Finally, it is important to measure and track the performance of your content so that you can optimize it for maximum impact.

Content marketing is an effective way to reach potential customers and build relationships with them. By creating content that is valuable and relevant, businesses can increase their visibility and reach more potential customers. Additionally, content marketing can help businesses build trust with their customers, as well as educate them on the products and services they offer. Content marketing is an essential part of any marketing strategy, and businesses should understand the benefits of content marketing and how to implement it effectively.

Section 2: Social Media Marketing

Social media marketing is an integral part of any modern marketing strategy. With the proliferation of social media platforms, there are more opportunities than ever to reach potential customers and build relationships with them.

Social media marketing involves creating content that is tailored to the platform, and then using that content to engage with the target audience. It can also involve leveraging existing relationships with customers to create word-of-mouth marketing.

One of the most important aspects of social media marketing is having an effective strategy. A successful strategy should be tailored to the platform, and should include elements such as content production, engagement, and analytics. Content production involves creating content that speaks to the target audience and is tailored to the platform. Engagement involves interacting with followers and driving conversations. Finally, analytics allow marketers to track results and make adjustments to their strategy as needed.

The goal of social media marketing is to build relationships with customers and drive sales. To do this, marketers must create content that resonates with their target audience. It's important to create content that is informative, entertaining, and relevant. Content should also be tailored to the platform, as different platforms have different audiences and different expectations.

In addition to creating content, marketers must also engage with their target audience. Engagement involves responding to comments, questions, and messages, as well as starting conversations. This helps to build relationships with customers and helps to keep them engaged with the brand.

Finally, marketers must track the results of their campaigns and use analytics to understand how their strategies are performing. Analytics can provide valuable insights into customer behavior, and can help marketers make adjustments to their strategies as needed.

Social media marketing is an essential part of any modern marketing strategy. With the right strategy and tactics, marketers can leverage the power of social media to build relationships with customers and drive sales.

Section 3: Pay-Per-Click Advertising

Pay-per-click (PPC) advertising is an online advertising model where advertisers pay a fee each time their ad is clicked. It is a way of buying visits to your website, rather than attempting to "earn" those visits organically. It is one of the most popular forms of digital marketing and is used by businesses of all sizes in virtually all industries.

PPC advertising is a type of sponsored online advertising that is used on a variety of websites and search engines. Advertisers bid on keywords that are relevant to their target market. When someone searches using one of these keywords, their ad may appear in the sponsored results section of the search engine. When someone clicks on their ad, they are directed to the advertiser's website and the advertiser pays the search engine a fee.

PPC advertising is highly targeted, allowing advertisers to reach people who are actively looking for their product or service. It is also highly measurable, so advertisers know exactly how much each click costs and how many people are clicking on their ad. This allows them to fine-tune their campaigns and get the best possible return on their investment.

One of the key benefits of PPC advertising is that it allows advertisers to reach their target market quickly and efficiently. With PPC, advertisers can set up their campaigns and start getting results almost immediately. Additionally, PPC campaigns can be set up in a relatively short period of time and require minimal setup and maintenance.

PPC advertising can be an effective way to increase traffic to your website and generate leads. It can also be used to reach a broader audience than organic search engine optimization. However, like any online marketing strategy, it is important to understand the basics and have a clear plan of action before launching a PPC campaign.

PPC advertising can be a great way to reach your target market quickly and efficiently. By understanding the basics of PPC and setting up a clear plan of action, you can maximize the return on your investment and get the most out of your PPC campaigns.

Chapter 6 of this book outlines several lead generation tactics that can be utilized to engage potential customers and increase sales. These tactics include creating content, using social media, running promotions, utilizing email campaigns, and using influencers. Each tactic is discussed in detail, highlighting its strengths and weaknesses and how it can be used to attract leads. It also provides tips on how to measure the effectiveness of each tactic and how to choose the right one for your business. Ultimately, this chapter provides a comprehensive overview of lead generation tactics and how they can help to increase sales.

Chapter 7: Final Thoughts

Chapter 7: Final Thoughts provides a concluding look at the concepts discussed in the book. It summarizes the main points of the book and explains the importance of understanding the concepts and applying them in life. It emphasizes how understanding and applying the material can help us to become successful, create meaningful relationships, and lead a more fulfilling life. It also serves as a reminder that we can always strive to be better. The book encourages us to be mindful of our actions and to use the knowledge we've gained to make better decisions. It is an important reminder that we all have the power to take control of our lives and improve ourselves if we are willing to put in the effort and do the work.

7: Final Thoughts

7: Final Thoughts is a book that encourages readers to take a step back and reflect on the various aspects of their lives. It is a collection of writings by author and philosopher John C. Maxwell that provide individuals with an opportunity to gain a greater understanding of their lives. Through these writings, readers are encouraged to take a deeper look at their values, goals, and motivations, and to consider how these can be used to create a more fulfilling life.

The book is divided into seven sections, each of which focuses on a particular aspect of life. These sections are broken down into topics such as faith, relationships, success, and purpose. Each section contains a number of short stories, anecdotes, and quotes that provide readers with a source of inspiration and motivation.

One of the main themes throughout the book is that of personal growth and development. Maxwell encourages readers to look beyond their current circumstances and to strive for a greater level of self-improvement. He encourages readers to take time to reflect on the decisions they have made and to consider how they could have been more effective. He also emphasizes the importance of having a strong foundation of values and principles, as this will provide the foundation for success in all areas of life.

The book also touches on the importance of relationships in life. Maxwell encourages readers to cultivate meaningful relationships with others and to prioritize these. He emphasizes the importance of making time for meaningful conversations, of listening to the perspective of others, and of investing in relationships. He also encourages readers to be mindful of how their relationships can impact their lives and to be mindful of how their own actions can affect these relationships.

Overall, 7: Final Thoughts provides readers with an opportunity to reflect on various aspects of their lives and to consider how they can make changes and pursue greater fulfillment. The short stories, anecdotes, and quotes provide readers with a source of inspiration and motivation and encourage them to take a look at their values, goals, and motivations. Through this book, readers can gain a greater understanding of their lives and can use this knowledge to create a more meaningful and fulfilling life.

Section 1: Summary of Lead Generation Strategies

Lead generation is the process of acquiring potential customers for a business. It's an essential part of any successful marketing strategy, and there are a variety of methods and tactics that businesses can use to generate leads. In order to maximize effectiveness, it's important to understand the different approaches and how they can be used to help you reach your goals.

One of the most common lead generation strategies is content marketing. This involves creating and sharing content such as blog posts, whitepapers, infographics, videos, and webinars that can be used to capture the attention of potential customers. Content should be relevant to the target audience and provide useful information in order to optimize lead generation.

Social media is another effective lead generation strategy. Platforms like Twitter, LinkedIn, and Facebook provide a great opportunity for businesses to reach out to potential customers by engaging with them through comments, likes, and shares. Content can be shared on these platforms as well, which can help to drive traffic to your website and increase the chances of gaining leads.

Search engine optimization (SEO) is also an important lead generation strategy. SEO involves optimizing content for search engines to help it rank higher in search engine results. This can drive more organic traffic to your website, which can lead to more leads.

Email marketing is another great lead generation strategy. It involves sending emails to potential customers with the goal of building relationships and converting them into leads. It's important to create an effective email campaign that resonates with the target audience and encourages them to take action.

Finally, paid advertisements can be an effective lead generation strategy. This involves using platforms like Google Ads, Facebook Ads, and LinkedIn Ads to reach potential customers and drive them to your website. This can be an expensive strategy, but it can be very effective if done correctly.

Lead generation is an important part of any successful marketing strategy. By understanding the different strategies and tactics available, businesses can create an effective lead generation strategy that will help them reach their goals. Content marketing, social media, SEO, email marketing, and paid advertising are all effective lead generation strategies that can be used to reach potential customers and increase the chances of gaining leads.

Section 2: Best Practices for Lead Generation

Lead generation is the process of identifying and nurturing prospective customers to turn them into paying customers. It's essential to a successful marketing strategy, and without it, your business will struggle to grow.

The key to effective lead generation is understanding the best practices that can help you maximize your success. Here are some of the best practices for lead generation:

1. Identify Your Target Audience

Before you start generating leads, you need to identify your target audience. You should have a clear understanding of who your ideal customers are and what their needs are. This will help you create targeted campaigns that are more likely to convert.

2. Utilize Multiple Lead Sources

Don't rely solely on one lead source. Utilize multiple sources to increase your chances of success. Consider using a combination of online and offline sources, such as email campaigns, social media, search engine optimization (SEO), and traditional marketing tactics.

3. Craft Compelling Content

Content is one of the most important elements of lead generation. Your content should be engaging and relevant to your target audience. Use visuals, videos, infographics, and other media to make your content stand out.

4. Offer Incentives

Offering incentives is a great way to encourage people to take action. Consider offering discounts, free trials, or other rewards to entice people to take the next step.

5. Use Automation

Automation can help you save time and energy while still providing a personalized experience to your leads. Automation tools can help you track engagement, segment leads, and send targeted emails.

6. Track and Analyze Your Results

Once you start generating leads, track your efforts to see what's working and what isn't. Analyze your results and use the data to adjust your strategies and optimize your efforts.

Lead generation is an essential part of any marketing strategy. By following these best practices, you can maximize your success and grow your business. Start using these tips today and start generating more leads and conversions.

Section 3: Tips for Scaling Your Lead Generation Efforts

As a business owner or marketer, the importance of lead generation cannot be understated. Without leads, your business will suffer; without leads, you won't make any sales. It's also important to note that the size of your database is only part of the equation – you also need to be able to generate quality leads.

If you want to maximize your lead generation efforts and generate more leads, it's important to keep the following tips in mind:

1. Focus on Content Marketing

Content marketing is one of the most effective and cost-efficient ways to generate leads. It involves creating and distributing content that's helpful and relevant to your target audience. This content can take many forms – blog posts, infographics, podcasts, ebooks, webinars, and more. By creating content that is valuable to your audience, you will be able to increase trust and build relationships with potential customers.

2. Leverage Social Media

Social media can be an incredibly powerful tool for lead generation. By creating an engaging presence on social media platforms, you can reach a wider audience and build relationships with potential customers. Make sure to post regularly and create content that is interesting and relevant to your target audience. Additionally, you can use social media to drive traffic to your website and blog, where you can capture leads through email opt-ins.

3. Utilize Automation

Automation can be a great way to scale your lead generation efforts. There are a variety of automation tools available, such as email marketing automation and lead scoring software. These tools can help you to nurture leads, segment your audience, and optimize your lead generation efforts.

These are just a few tips for scaling your lead generation efforts. The key is to create a comprehensive lead generation strategy that focuses on content marketing, social media, and automation. By doing this, you will be able to increase your leads and maximize your return on investment.

Good luck!

Chapter 7: Final Thoughts is a great way to wrap up a book, as it provides an opportunity to reflect on the main points and summarize the key takeaways. This chapter can also be used to consider any unanswered questions, as well as to suggest further reading or other resources to explore. Finally, it's an ideal time to thank readers for their attention and offer them a chance to provide feedback or to contact the author for further questions. It's a great way to end a book and leave readers with a lasting impression.

More of our books

The Product Marketing Manager Handbook

Are you ready to unlock the secrets of successful product marketing in the digital age? Look no further! "The Product Marketing Manager Handbook" is your ultimate guide to navigating the complex landscape of product marketing and driving tangible results.

The Marketing Coordinator Handbook

Are you ready to unlock your full potential as a marketing coordinator? Look no further than "The Marketing Coordinator Handbook" – the ultimate guide to mastering the art of marketing coordination. This comprehensive book is designed to equip aspiring and current marketing coordinators with the essential knowledge, skills, and strategies needed to excel in their roles and drive remarkable results.

The Social Media Manager Handbook

"The Social Media Manager Handbook" is an indispensable guide for aspiring and experienced social media managers who want to excel in their roles and make a significant impact on their organization's digital presence. This comprehensive handbook covers everything from fundamental concepts to advanced strategies, equipping readers with the knowledge and skills needed to navigate the dynamic and ever-changing landscape of social media.

The Marketing Manager Handbook

Introducing "The Marketing Manager Handbook," a definitive guide designed to equip marketing professionals with the essential skills, knowledge, and strategies needed to excel in their role. This comprehensive book serves as a trusted companion, providing valuable insights and practical advice for marketing managers across various industries.

Printed in Dunstable, United Kingdom